Ballads & Lyrics of Old France

Andrew Lang

Contents

BALLADS & LYRICS OF OLD FRANCE

BY

Andrew Lang

LIST OF POETS TRANSLATED

I CHARLES D'ORLEANS, who has sometimes, for no very obvious reason, been styled the father of French lyric poetry, was born in May, 1391. He was the son of Louis D'Orleans, the grandson of Charles V., and the father of Louis XII. Captured at Agincourt, he was kept in England as a prisoner from 1415 to 1440, when he returned to France, where he died in 1465. His verses, for the most part roundels on two rhymes, are songs of love and spring, and retain the allegorical forms of the Roman de la Rose.

II. FRANÇOIS VILLON, 1431-14—? Nothing is known of Villon's birth or death, and only too much of his life. In his poems the ancient forms of French verse are animated with the keenest sense of personal emotion, of love, of melancholy, of mocking despair, and of repentance for a life passed in taverns and prisons.

III. JOACHIM DU BELLAY, 1525-1560. The exact date of Du Bellay's birth is unknown. He was certainly a little younger than Ronsard, who was born in September, 1524, although an attempt has been made to prove that his birth took place in 1525, as a compensation from Nature to France for the battle of Pavia. As a poet Du Bellay had the start, by a few months, of Ronsard; his Recueil was published in 1549. The question of priority in the new style of poetry caused a quarrel, which did not long separate the two singers. Du Bellay is perhaps the most interesting of the Pleiad, that company of Seven, who attempted to reform French verse, by inspiring it with the enthusiasm of the Renaissance. His book L'Illustration de la langue Française is a plea for the study of ancient models and for the improvement of the vernacular. In this effort Du Bellay and Ronsard are the predecessors of Malherbe, and of André Chénier, more successful through their frank eagerness than the former, less fortunate in the possession of critical learning and appreciative taste than the latter. There is something in Du Bellay's life, in the artistic nature checked by occupation in affairs—he was the secretary of Cardinal Du Bellay—in the regret and affection with which Rome depressed and allured him, which reminds the English reader of the thwarted career of Clough.

IV. REMY BELLEAU, 1528-1577. Du Belleau's life was spent in the household of Charles de Lor raine, Marquis d'Elboeuf, and was marked by nothing more eventful than the usual pilgrimage to Italy, the sacred land and sepulchre of art.

V. PIERRE RONSARD, 1524-1585. Ronsard's early years gave little sign of his vocation. He was for some time a page of the court, was in the serviceof James V. of Scotland, and had his share of shipwrecks, battles, and amorous adventures. An illness which produced total deafness made him a scholar and poet, as in another age and country it might have made him a saint and an ascetic. With all his industry, and almost religious zeal for art, he is one of the poets who make themselves, rather than are born singers. His epic, the Franciade, is as tedious as other artificial epics, and his odes are almost unreadable. We are never allowed to forget that he is the poet who read the Iliad through in three days. He is, as has been said of Le Brun, more mythological than Pindar. His constant allusion to his grey hair, an affectation which may be noticed in Shelley, is borrowed from Anacreon. Many of the sonnets in which he " petrarquizes," retain the faded odour of the roses he loved ; and his songs have fire and melancholy and a sense as of perfume from "a closet long to quiet vowed, with mothed and dropping arras hung." Ronsard's great fame declined when Malherbe came to "bind the sweet influences of the Pleiad," but he has been duly honoured by the newest school of French poetry.

VI. JACQUES TAHUREAU, 1 527-1555. The amorous poetry of Jacques Tahureau has the merit, rare in his, or in any age, of being the real expression of passion. His brief life burned itself away before he had exhausted the lyric effusion of his youth. " Le plus beau gentilhomme de son siécle, et le plus dextre . à toutes sortes de gentillesses," died at the age of twenty-eight, fulfilling the presentiment which tinges, but scarcely saddens his poetry.

VII. JEAN PASSERAT, I534-1602. Better known as a political satirist than as a poet.

POETS OF THE NINETEENTH CENTURY

VICTOR HUGO.
ALFRED DE MUSSET, 1810-1857.
GÈRARD DE NERVAL, 1801-1855.
HENRI MURGER, 1822-1861.
BALLADS

The originals of the French folk-songs here translated are to be found in the collections of MM. De Puymaigre and Gerard de Nerval, and in the report of M. Ampere.

The verses called a "Lady of High Degree" are imitated from a very early chanson in Bartsch's collection.

The Greek ballads have been translated with the aid of the French versions by M. Fauriel.
SPRING

CHARLES D'ORLEANS, 1391-1465
The new-liveried year.—*Sir Henry Wotlon*

THE year has changed his mantle cold Of wind, of rain, of bitter air;
And he goes clad in cloth of gold,
Of laughing suns and season fair;
No bird or beast of wood or wold
But doth with cry or song declare
The year lays down his mantle cold.
All founts, all rivers, seaward rolled,

The pleasant summer livery wear,
With silver studs on broidered vair;
The world puts off its raiment old,
The year lays down his mantle cold.

RONDEL

CHARLES D'ORLEANS, 1 391-1465

To his Mistress, to succour his heart that is beleaguered by jealousy

STRENGTHEN, my Love, this castle of my heart,
And with some store of pleasure give me aid,
For Jealousy, with all them of his part,
Strong siege about the weary tower has laid.
Nay, if to break his bands thou art afraid,
Too weak to make his cruel force depart,
Strengthen at least this castle of my heart,
And with some store of pleasure give me aid.
Nay, let not Jealousy, for all his art
Be master, and the tower in ruin laid,
That still, ah Love ! thy gracious rule obeyed.
Advance, and give me succour of thy part;
Strengthen, my Love, this castle of my heart.

FRANÇOIS VILLON, 1460
GOOD-BYE ! the tears are in my eyes;
Farewell, farewell, my prettiest;
Farewell, of women born the best
Good-bye ! the saddest of good-byes
Farewell! with many vows and sighs
My sad heart leaves you to your rest
Farewell! the tears are in my eyes;

Farewell! from you my miseries
Are more than now may be confessed,
And most by thee have I been blessed,
Yea, and for thee have wasted sighs;
Good-bye ! the last of my good-byes.

ARBOR AMORIS

FRANÇOIS VILLON, 1460

I HAVE a tree, a graft of Love,
That in my heart has taken root; Sad
are the buds and blooms thereof,
And bitter sorrow is its fruit;
Yet, since it was a tender shoot, So
greatly hath its shadow spread,
That underneath all joy is dead,
And all my pleasant days are flown,
Nor can I slay it, nor instead
Plant any tree, save this alone.

Ah, yet, for long and long enough
My tears were rain about its root,
And though the fruit be harsh thereof,
I scarcely looked for better fruit
Than this, that carefully I put In
garner, for the bitter bread
Whereon my weary life is fed:
Ah, better were the soil unsown That bears
such growths; but Love instead
Will plant no tree, but this alone.

Ah, would that this new spring, whereof The

leaves and flowers flush into shoot,
I might have succour and aid of Love
To
prune these branches at the root, That
long
have borne such bitter fruit,
And graft a new bough, comforted
With happy blossoms white and red; So
pleasure should for pain atone,
Nor Love slay this tree, nor instead Plant
any tree, but this alone.
Princess, by whom my hope is fed,
My heart thee prays in lowlihead
To prune the ill boughs overgrown,
Nor slay Love's tree, nor plant instead
Another tree, save this alone.

BALLAD OF THE GIBBET

An epitaph in the form of a ballad that François Villon wrote of himself and his company, they expecting shortly to be hanged

BROTHERS and men that shall after us be,
Let not your hearts be hard to us:
For pitying this our misery
Ye shall find God the more piteous.
Look on us six that are hanging thus,
And for the flesh that so much we cherished
How it is eaten of birds and perished,
And ashes and dust fill our bones' place,
Mock not at us that so feeble be,
But pray God pardon us out of His grace.

Listen, we pray you, and look not in scorn, Though
justly, in sooth, we are cast to die;
Ye wot no man so wise is born
That keeps his wisdom constantly.
Be ye then merciful, and cry
To Mary's Son that is piteous,
 That His mercy take no stain from us,
Saving us out of the fiery place.
We are but dead, let no soul deny
To pray God succour us of His grace.

The rain out of heaven has washed us clean,
The sun has scorched us black and bare,
 Ravens and rooks have pecked at our eyne,
And feathered their nests with our beards and hair.
Round are we tossed, and here and there,
This way and that, at the wild wind's will,
Never a moment my body is still;
Birds they are busy about my face.
Live not as we, nor fare as we fare;
Pray God pardon us out of His Grace.
Prince Jesus, Master of all, to thee
We pray Hell gain no mastery,
That we come never anear that place;
And ye men, make no mockery,
Pray God pardon us out of His grace.

HYMN TO THE WINDS

The winds are invoked by the winnowers of corn

Du BELLAY, 1550

To you, troop so fleet,
That with winged wandering feet,
Through the wide world pass,
And with soft murmuring
Toss the green shades of spring
In woods and grass,
Lily and violet
I give, and blossoms wet,
Roses and dew;
This branch of blushing roses,
Whose fresh bud uncloses,
Wind-flowers too.
Ah, winnow with sweet breath,
Winnow the holt and heath,
Round this retreat;
Where all the golden morn
We fan the gold o' the corn,
In the sun's heat.

A VOW TO HEAVENLY VENUS

Du BELLAY, 1550

WE that with like hearts love, we lovers twain,
New wedded in the village by thy fane,
Lady of all chaste love, to thee it is
We bring these amaranths, these white lilies,
A sign, and sacrifice; may Love, we pray,
Like amaranthine flowers, feel no decay;
Like these cool lilies may our loves remain,
Perfect and pure, and know not any stain;
And be our hearts, from this thy holy hour,
Bound each to each, like flower to wedded

flower.

TO HIS FRIEND IN ELYSIUM

Du BELLAY, 1550

So long you wandered on the dusky plain,
Where flit the shadows with their endless
cry, You reach the shore where all the world goes by,
You leave the strife, the slavery, the pain;
But we, but we, the mortals that remain
In vain stretch hands; for Charon sullenly
Drives us afar, we may not come anigh
Till that last mystic obolus we gain.

But you are happy in the quiet place,
And with the learned lovers of old days,
And with your love, you wander evermore
In the dim woods, and drink forgetfulness
Of us your friends, a weary crowd that press
About the gate, or labour at the oar.

A SONNET TO HEAVENLY BEAUTY

Du BELLAY, 1550

IF this our little life is but a day
In the Eternal,—if the years in vain
Toil after hours that never come again,—
If everything that hath been must decay,
Why dreamest thou of joys that pass away,
My soul, that my sad body doth restrain ?
Why of the moment's pleasure art thou fain ?

Nay, thou hast wings,—nay, seek another stay.

There is the joy whereto each soul aspires,
And there the rest that all the world desires,
And there is love, and peace, and gracious mirth;
And there in the most highest heavens shalt
thou
Behold the Very Beauty, whereof now
Thou worshippest the shadow upon earth.

APRIL

REMY BELLEAU, 1560

APRIL, pride of woodland ways,
Of glad days,
April, bringing hope of prime,
To the young flowers that beneath
Their bud sheath
Are guarded in their tender time;

April, pride of fields that be
Green and free,
That in fashion glad and gay,
Stud with flowers red and blue,
Every hue,
Their jewelled spring array;

April, pride of murmuring
Winds of spring,
That beneath the winnowed air,
Trap with subtle nets and sweet
Flora's feet,

Flora's feet, the fleet and fair;

April, by thy hand caressed,
From her breast
Nature scatters everywhere
Handfuls of all sweet perfumes,
Buds and blooms,
Making faint the earth and air.

April, joy of the green hours,
Clothes with flowers
Over all her locks of gold
My sweet Lady; and her breast
With the blest
Buds of summer manifold.

April, with thy gracious wiles,
Like the smiles,
Smiles of Venus; and thy breath
Like her breath, the Gods' delight,
(From their height
They take the happy air beneath;)

It is thou that, of thy grace,
From their place
In the far-off isles dost bring
Swallows over earth and sea,
Glad to be
Messengers of thee, and Spring.

Daffodil and eglantine,
And woodbine,
Lily, violet, and rose

Plentiful in April fair,
To the air,
Their pretty petals do unclose.

Nightingales ye now may hear,
Piercing clear,
Singing in the deepest shade;
Many and many a babbled note
Chime and float,
Woodland music through the glade.

April, all to welcome thee,
Spring sets free
Ancient flames, and with low breath
Wakes the ashes grey and old
That the cold
Chilled within our hearts to death.

Thou beholdest in the warm
Hours, the swarm
Of the thievish bees, that flies
Evermore from bloom to bloom
For perfume,
Hid away in tiny thighs.

Her cool shadows May can boast,
Fruits almost
Ripe, and gifts of fertile dew,
Manna-sweet and honey-sweet,
That complete
Her flower garland fresh and new.

Nay, but I will give my praise,

To these days,
Named with the glad name of Her [1]
That from out the foam o' the sea
Came to be
Sudden light on earth and air.

[1] Aphrodite—Avril

ROSES

RONSARD, 1550

I SEND you here a wreath of blossoms blown,
And woven flowers at sunset gatherèd,
Another dawn had seen them ruined, and shed
Loose leaves upon the grass at random strown.
By this, their sure example, be it known,
That all your beauties, now in perfect flower,
Shall fade as these, and wither in an hour,
Flowerlike, and brief of days, as the flower sown.
Ah, time is flying, lady—time is flying;
Nay, 'tis not time that flies but we that go,
Who in short space shall be in churchyard lying,
And of our loving parley none shall know,
Nor any man consider what we were;
Be therefore kind, my love, whiles thou art fair.

THE ROSE

RONSARD, 1550

SEE, Mignonne, hath not the Rose,
That this morning did unclose
Her purple mantle to the light,
Lost, before the day be dead,
The glory of her raiment red,
Her colour, bright as yours is bright ?

Ah, Mignonne, in how few hours,
The petals of her purple flowers
All have faded, fallen, died;
Sad Nature, mother ruinous,.
That seest thy fair child perish thus.
'Twixt matin song and even-tide.

Hear me, my darling, speaking sooth,
Gather the fleet flower of your youth,
Take ye your pleasure at the best;
Be merry ere your beauty flit,
For length of days will tarnish it
Like roses that were loveliest.

TO THE MOON

RONSARD, 1550

HIDE this one night thy crescent, kindly Moon;
So shall Endymion faithful prove, and rest
Loving and unawakened on thy breast;

So shall no foul enchanter importune
Thy quiet course; for now the night is boon,
And through the friendly night unseen I fare,
Who dread the face of foemen unaware,
And watch of hostile spies in the bright noon.
Thou knowest, Moon, the bitter power of Love;
'Tis told how shepherd Pan found ways to move,
For little price, thy heart; and of your grace,
Sweet stars, be kind to this not alien fire,
Because on earth ye did not scorn desire,
Bethink ye, now ye hold your heavenly place.

TO HIS YOUNG MISTRESS

RONSARD, 1550

FAIR flower of fifteen springs, that still
Art scarcely blossomed from the bud,
Yet hast such store of evil will,
A heart so full of hardihood,
Seeking to hide in friendly wise
The mischief of your mocking eyes.

If you have pity, child, give o'er;
Give back the heart you stole from me,
Pirate, setting so little store
On this your captive from Love's sea,
Holding his misery for gain,
And making pleasure of his pain.

Another, not so fair of face,
But far more pitiful than you,
Would take my heart, if of his grace,

My heart would give her of Love's due;
And she shall have it, since I find
That you are cruel and unkind.

Nay, I would rather that it died,
Within your white hands prisoning,
Would rather that it still abide
In your ungentle comforting,
Than change its faith, and seek to her
That is more kind, but not so fair.

DEADLY KISSES

RONSARD, 1550

AH take these lips away; no more,
No more such kisses give to me.
My spirit faints for joy; I see
Through mists of death the dreamy shore,
And meadows by the water-side,
Where all about the Hollow Land
Fare the sweet singers that have died,
With their lost ladies, hand in hand;
Ah, Love, how fireless are their eyes,
How pale their lips that kiss and smile!
So mine must be in little while
If thou wilt kiss me in such wise.

OF HIS LADY'S OLD AGE

RONSARD, I550

WHEN you are very old, at evening
You'll sit and spin beside the fire, and say,
Humming my songs, " Ah well, ah well-a-day!
When I was young, of me did Ronsard sing."
None of your maidens that doth hear the thing,
Albeit with her weary task foredone,
But wakens at my name, and calls you one
Blest, to be held in long remembering.

I shall be low beneath the earth, and laid
On sleep, a phantom in the myrtle shade,
While you beside the fire, a grandame grey,
My love, your pride, remember and regret;
Ah, love me, love! we may be happy yet,
And gather roses, while 'tis called to-day.

ON HIS LADY'S WAKING

RONSARD, 1550

MY lady woke upon a morning fair,
What time Apollo's chariot takes the skies,
And, fain to fill with arrows from her eyes
His empty quiver, Love was standing there:
I saw two apples that her breast doth bear
None such the close of the Hesperides
Yields; nor hath Venus any such as these,

Nor she that had of nursling Mars the care.

Even such a bosom, and so fair it was,
Pure as the perfect work of Phidias,
That sad Andromeda's discomfiture
Left bare, when Perseus passed her on a day,
And pale as Death for fear of Death she lay,
With breast as marble cold, as marble pure.

HIS LADY'S DEATH

RONSARD, 1550

TWAIN that were foes, while Mary lived, are fled;
One laurel-crowned abides in heaven, and one
Beneath the earth has fared, a fallen sun,
A light of love among the loveless dead.
The first is Chastity, that vanquishèd
The archer Love, that held joint empery
With the sweet beauty that made war on me,
When laughter of lips with laughing eyes was wed.

Their strife the Fates have closed, with stern
control,
The earth holds her fair body, and her soul
An angel with glad angels triumpheth;
Love has no more that he can do; desire
Is buried, and my heart a faded fire,
And for Death's sake, I am in love with Death.

HIS LADY'S TOMB

RONSARD, 1550

As in the gardens, all through May, the rose,
Lovely, and young, and fair apparelled,
Makes sunrise jealous of her rosy red,
When dawn upon the dew of dawning glows;
Graces and Loves within her breast repose,
The woods are faint with the sweet odour shed,
Till rains and heavy suns have smitten dead
The languid flower, and the loose leaves unclose,—
So this, the perfect beauty of our days,
When earth and heaven were vocal of her praise,
The fates have slain, and her sweet soul
reposes;
And tears I bring, and sighs, and on her tomb
Pour milk, and scatter buds of many a bloom,
That dead, as living, she may be with roses.

SHADOWS OF HIS LADY

JACQUES TAHUREAU, 1527-1555

WITHIN the sand of what far river lies
The gold that gleams in tresses of my Love?
What highest circle of the Heavens above
Is jewelled with such stars as are her eyes ?
And where is the rich sea whose coral vies
With her red lips, that cannot kiss enough ?
What dawn-lit garden knew the rose, whereof

The fled soul lives in her cheeks' rosy guise ?

What Parian marble that is loveliest,
Can match the whiteness of her brow and breast
When drew she breath from the Sabæan
glade ?
Oh happy rock and river, sky and sea,
Gardens, and glades Sabæan, all that be
The far-off splendid semblance of my maid!

MOONLIGHT

JACQUES TAHUREAU, 1527-1555

THE high Midnight was garlanding her head
With many a shining star in shining skies,
And, of her grace, a slumber on mine eyes,
And, after sorrow, quietness was shed.
Far in dim fields cicalas jargonèd
A thin shrill clamour of complaints and cries;
And all the woods were pallid, in strange wise,
With pallor of the sad moon overspread.

Then came my lady to that lonely place,
And, from her palfrey stooping, did embrace
And hang upon my neck, and kissed me over;
Wherefore the day is far less dear than night,
And sweeter is the shadow than the light,
Since night has made me such a happy lover.

LOVE IN MAY

PASSERAT, 1580

OFF with sleep, love, up from bed,
This fair morn;
See, for our eyes the rosy red
New dawn is born;
Now that skies are glad and gay
In this gracious month of May,
Love me, sweet,
Fill my joy in brimming measure,
In this world he hath no pleasure,
That will none of it.

Come, love, through the woods of spring,
Come walk with me;
Listen, the sweet birds jargoning
From tree to tree.

List and listen, over all
Nightingale most musical
That ceases never; Grief
begone, and let us be
For a space as glad as he;
Time's flitting ever.

Old Time, that loves not lovers, wears
Wings swift in flight;
All our happy life he bears
Far in the night.
Old and wrinkled on a day,

Sad and weary shall you say,
" Ah, fool was I,
That took no pleasure in the grace
Of the flower that from my face
Time has seen die."

Leave then sorrow, teen, and tears
Till we be old;
Young we are, and of our years
Till youth be cold

Pluck the flower; while spring is gay
In this happy month of May
Love me, love;
Fill our joy in brimming measure;
 In this world he hath no pleasure
That will none thereof.

THE GRAVE AND THE ROSE

VICTOR HUGO

THE Grave said to the Rose,
" What of the dews of dawn,
Love's flower, what end is theirs ?"
"And what of spirits flown,
The souls whereon doth close
The tomb's mouth unawares ? "
The Rose said to the Grave.

The Rose said, "In the shade
From the dawn's tears is made
A perfume faint and strange,
Amber and honey sweet."

" And all the spirits fleet
Do suffer a sky-change,
More strangely than the dew,
To God's own angels new,"
The Grave said to the Rose.

THE GENESIS OF BUTTERFLIES

VICTOR HUGO

THE dawn is smiling on the dew that covers
The tearful roses; lo, the little lovers
That kiss the buds, and all the fluttering
In jasmine bloom, and privet, of white wings,
That go and come, and fly, and peep and
hide,
With muffled music, murmured far and wide!
Ah, Spring time, when we think of all the lays
That dreamy lovers send to dreamy mays,
Of the fond hearts within a billet bound,
Of all the soft silk paper that pens wound,
The messages of love that mortals write
Filled with intoxication of delight,
Written in April, and before the May time
Shredded and flown, playthings for the wind's
playtime,

We dream that all white butterflies above,
Who seek through clouds or waters souls to love,
And leave their lady mistress in despair,
To flit to flowers, as kinder and more fair,
Are but torn love-letters, that through the skies

Flutter, and float, and change to Butterflies.

MORE STRONG THAN TIME

VICTOR HUGO

SINCE I have set my lips to your full cup, my sweet,
Since I my pallid face between your hands have laid,
Since I have known your soul, and all the bloom of it,
And all the perfume rare, 'now buried in the shade;
Since it was given to me to hear one happy while,
The words wherein your heart spoke all its mysteries,

Since I have seen you weep, and since I have seen you smile,
Your lips upon my lips, and your eyes upon my eyes;
Since I have known above my forehead glance and gleam,
A ray, a single ray, of your star, veiled always,
Since I have felt the fall, upon my lifetime's stream,
Of one rose petal plucked from the roses of your days;

I now am bold to say to the swift changing hours,
Pass, pass upon your way, for I grow never old,
Fleet to the dark abysm with all your fading
flowers,
One rose that none may pluck, within my heart
I hold.

Your flying wings may smite, but they can never spill
 The cup fulfilled of love, from which my lips are wet;
My heart has far more fire than you have frost to chill,
My soul more love than you can make my soul forget.

AN OLD TUNE

GÈRARD DE NERVAL

THERE is an air for which I would disown
Mozart's, Rossini's, Weber's melodies,—
A sweet sad air that languishes and sighs,
And keeps its secret charm for me alone.

Whene'er I hear that music vague and old,
Two hundred years are mist that rolls away;
The thirteenth Louis reigns, and I behold
A green land golden in the dying day.

An old red castle, strong with stony towers,
The windows gay with many coloured glass;
Wide plains, and rivers flowing among flowers,
That bathe the castle basement as they pass,

In antique weed, with dark eyes and gold hair,
A lady looks forth from her window high;
It may be that I knew and found her fair,
In some forgotten life, long time gone by.

JUAN A

ALFRED DE MUSSET

AGAIN I see you, ah my queen,
Of all my old loves that have been,
The first love, and the tenderest;

Do you remember or forget—
Ah me, for I remember yet—
How the last summer days were blest ?

Ah lady, when we think of this,
The foolish hours of youth and bliss,
How fleet, how sweet, how hard to hole
How old we are, ere spring be green !
You touch the limit of eighteen
And I am twenty winters old.

My rose, that mid the red roses,
Was brightest, ah, how pale she is!
Yet keeps the beauty of her prime;
Child, never Spanish lady's face
Was lovely with so wild a grace;
Remember the dead summer time.

Think of our loves, our feuds of old,
And how you gave your chain of gold
To me for a peace offering;
And how all night I lay awake
To touch and kiss it for your sake,—
To touch and kiss the lifeless thing.

Lady, beware, for all we say,
This Love shall live another day,
Awakened from his deathly sleep;
The heart that once has been your shrine
For other loves is too divine;
A home, my dear, too wide and deep.

What did I say—why do I dream ?

Why should 1 struggle with the stream
Whose waves return not any day ?
Close heart, and eyes, and arms from me;
Farewell, farewell! so must it be,
So runs, so runs, the world away.

The season bears upon its wing
The swallows and the songs of spring,
And days that were, and days that flit
The loved lost hours are far away;
And hope and fame are scattered spray
For me, that gave you love a day
For you that not remember it.

SPRING IN THE STUDENT'S QUARTER

HENRI MURGER

WINTER is passing, and the bells
For ever with their silver lay
Murmur a melody that tells
Of April and of Easter day.
High in sweet air the light vane sets,
The weathercocks all southward twirl;
A sou will buy her violets
And make Nini a happy girl.

The winter to the poor was sore,
Counting the weary winter days,
Watching his little firewood store,
The bitter snowflakes fell always;

And now his last log dimly gleamed,

Lighting the room with feeble glare,
Half cinder and half smoke it seemed
That the wind wafted into air.

Pilgrims from ocean and far isles
See where the east is reddening,
The flocks that fly a thousand miles
From sunsetting to sunsetting ;
Look up, look out, behold the swallows,
The throats that twitter, the wings that beat;

And on their song the summer follows,
And in the summer life is sweet.

With the green tender buds that know
The shoot and sap of lusty spring
My neighbour of a year ago
Her casement, see, is opening;

Through all the bitter months that were,
Forth from her nest she dared not flee,
She was a study for Boucher,
She now might sit to Gavarni.

OLD LOVES

HENRI MURGER

LOUISE, have you forgotten yet
The corner of the flowery land,
The ancient garden where we met,
My hand that trembled in your hand ?
Our lips found words scarce sweet enough,

As low beneath the willow-trees
We sat; have you forgotten, love ?
Do you remember, love Louise ?

Marie, have you forgotten yet
The loving barter that we made ?
The rings we changed, the suns that set,
The woods fulfilled with sun and shade ?

The fountains that were musical
By many an ancient trysting tree—
Marie, have you forgotten all ?
Do you remember, love Marie ?

Christine, do you remember yet
Your room with scents and roses gay ?
My garret—near the sky 'twas set—
The April hours, the nights of May ?
The clear calm nights—the stars above
That whispered they were fairest seen
Through no cloud-veil ? Remember, love !
Do you remember, love Christine ?

Louise is dead, and, well-a-day!
Marie a sadder path has ta'en;
And pale Christine has passed away
In southern suns to bloom again.

Alas! for one and all of us—
Marie, Louise, Christine forget;
Our bower of love is ruinous,
And I alone remember yet.

MUSETTE

HENRI MURGER, 1850
YESTERDAY, watching the swallows' flight
That bring the spring and the season fair,
A moment I thought of the beauty bright
Who loved me, when she had time to spare;
And dreamily, dreamily all the day,
I mused on the calendar of the year,
The year so near and so far away,
When you were lief, and when I was dear.

Your memory has not had time to pass;
My youth has days of its lifetime yet;
If you only knocked at the door, alas,
My heart would open the door, Musette!
Still at your name must my sad heart beat;
Ah Muse, ah maiden of faithlessness !
Return for a moment, and deign to eat
The bread that pleasure was wont to bless.

The tables and curtains, the chairs and all,
Friends of our pleasure that looked on our pain
Are glad with the gladness of festival,
Hoping to see you at home again;
Come, let the days of their mourning pass,
The silent friends that are sad for you yet;
The little sofa, the great wine glass—
For know you had often my share, Musette.

Come, you shall wear the raiment white
You wore of old, when the world was gay,

We will wander in woods of the heart's delight
The whole of the Sunday holiday.
Come, we will sit by the wayside inn,
Come, and your song will gain force to fly,
Dipping its wing in the clear and thin
Wine, as of old, ere it scale the sky.

Musette, who had scarcely forgotten withal
One beautiful dawn of the new year's best,
Returned at the end of the carnival,
A flown bird, to a forsaken nest.

Ah faithless and fair ! I embrace her yet,
With no heart-beat, and with never a sigh;
And Musette, no longer the old Musette,
Declares that I am no longer I.

Farewell, my dear that was once so dear,
Dead with the death of our latest love;
Our youth is laid in its sepulchre,
The calendar stands for a stone above.
Tis only in searching the dust of the days,
The ashes of all old memories,
That we find the key of the woodland ways
That lead to the place of our paradise.

BALLADS

THE THREE CAPTAINS

ALL beneath the white-rose tree
Walks a lady fair to see,
She is as white as the snows,

She is as fair as the day :
From her father's garden close
Three knights have ta'en her away.

He has ta'en her by the hand,
The youngest of the three—
" Mount and ride, my bonnie bride,
On my white horse with me."

And ever they rode, and better rode,
Till they came to Senlis town,
The hostess she looked hard at them
As they were lighting down.

" And are ye here by force," she said,
" Or are ye here for play ? "
" From out my father's garden close
Three knights me stole away.

" And fain would I win back," she said,
" The weary way I come ;
And fain would see my father dear,
And fain go maiden home."

" Oh, weep not, lady fair," said she,
" You shall win back," she said,
" For you shall take this draught from me
Will make you lie for dead."

" Come in and sup, fair lady," they said,
" Come busk ye and be bright;
It is with three bold captains
That ye must be this night."

When they had eaten well and drunk,
She fell down like one slain:"
Now, out and alas! for my bonny may
Shall live no more again."

" Within her father's garden stead
There are three white lilies;
With her body to the lily bed,
With her soul to Paradise."

They bore her to her father's house,
They bore her all the three,
They laid her in her father's close,
Beneath the white-rose tree.
She had not lain a day, a day,
A day but barely three,
When the may awakes, " Oh, open, father,
Oh, open the door for me.

" ' Tis I have lain for dead, father
Have lain the long days three,
That I might maiden come again
To my mother and to thee."

THE BRIDGE OF DEATH

" THE dance is on the Bridge of Death
 And who will dance with me?"
" There's never a man of living men
Will dare to dance with thee."

Now Margaret's gone within her bower

Put ashes in her hair,
And sackcloth on her bonny breast,
And on her shoulders bare.

There came a knock to her bower door,
And blithe she let him in;
It was her brother from the wars,
The dearest of her kin.

" Set gold within your hair, Margaret,
Set gold within your hair,
And gold upon your girdle band,
And on your breast so fair.

For we are bidden to dance to-night,
We may not bide away,
This one good night, this one fair night,
Before the red new day."

" Nay, no gold for my head, brother,
Nay, no gold for my hair;
It is the ashes and dust of earth
That you and I must wear.

" No gold work for my girdle band,
No gold work on my feet;
But ashes of the fire, my love,
But dust that the serpents eat."

They danced across the Bridge of Death,
Above the black water,
And the marriage-bell was tolled in hell
For the souls of him and her.

LE PÈRE SÈVÈRE

KING LOUIS' DAUGHTER

BALLAD OF THE ISLE OF FRANCE

KING LOUIS on his bridge is he, He
holds his daughter on his knee.

She asks a husband at his hand
That is not worth a rood of land.

" Give up your lover speedily,
Or you within the tower must lie."

" Although I must the prison dree,
I will not change my love for thee.

" I will not change my lover fair
Not for the mother that me bare.

" I will not change my true lover
For friends, or for my father dear."

" Now where are all my pages keen,
And where are all my serving men ?

"My daughter must lie in the tower alway,
Where she shall never see the day."

Seven long years are past and gone
And there has seen her never one.

At ending of the seventh year
Her father goes to visit her.

" My child, my child, how may you be?"
" O father, it fares ill with me.

" My feet are wasted in the mould,
The worms they gnaw my side so cold."

" My child, change your love speedily
Or you must still in prison lie."

"Tis better far the cold to dree
Than give my true love up for thee."

THE MILK WHITE DOE

IT was a mother and a maid
That walked the woods among,
And still the maid went slow and sad,
And still the mother sung.

" What ails you, daughter Margaret ?
Why go you pale and wan ?
Is it for a cast of bitter love,
Or for a false leman ? "

" It is not for a false lover
That I go sad to see;
But it is for a weary life
Beneath the greenwood tree.

" For ever in the good daylight
A maiden may I go,
 But always on the ninth midnight
I change to a milk white doe.

" They hunt me through the green forest
With hounds and hunting men;
And ever it is my fair brother
That is so fierce and keen."

" Good-morrow, mother." " Good-morrow, son;
Where are your hounds so good ? "
" Oh, they are hunting a white doe
Within the glad greenwood.

" And three times have they hunted her,
And thrice she's won away ;
The fourth time that they follow her
That white doe they shall slay."

Then out and spoke the forester,
As he came from the wood,
" Now never saw I maid's gold hair
Among the wild deer's blood.

" And I have hunted the wild deer
In east lands and in west;
And never saw I white doe yet
That had a maiden's breast."

Then up and spake her fair brother,
Between the wine and bread,
" Behold, I had but one sister,

And I have been her dead."

" But ye must bury my sweet sister
With a stone at her foot and her head,
And ye must cover her fair body
With the white roses and red."

And I must out to the greenwood,
The roof shall never shelter me;
And I shall lie for seven long years
On the grass below the hawthorn tree.

A LADY OF HIGH DEGREE

I be pareld most of prise,
I ride after the wild fee.
WILL ye that I should sing
Of the love of a goodly thing,
Was no vilein's may ?
Tis sung of a knight so free,
Under the olive tree,
Singing this lay.

Her weed was of samite fine,
Her mantle of white ermine,
Green silk her hose;
Her shoon with silver gay,
Her sandals flowers of May,
Laced small and close.

Her belt was of fresh spring buds,
Set with gold clasps and studs,
Fine linen her shift;

Her purse it was of love,
Her chain was the flower thereof,
And Love's gift.

Upon a mule she rode,
The selle was of brent gold,
The bits of silver made;
Three red rose trees there were
That overshadowed her,
For a sun shade.

She riding on a day,
Knights met her by the way,
They did her grace;
" Fair lady, whence be ye ? "
" France it is my countrie,
I come of a high race.

" My sire is the nightingale,
That sings, making his wail,
In the wild wood, clear;
The mermaid is mother to me,
That sings in the salt sea,
In the ocean mere."

" Ye come of a right good race,
And are born of a high place,
And of high degree;
Would to God that ye were
Given unto me, being fair,
My lady and love to be."

LOST FOR A ROSE'S SAKE

I LAVED my hands,
By the water side;
With the willow leaves
My hands I dried.

The nightingale sung
On the bough of the tree;
Sing, sweet nightingale,
It is well with thee.

Thou hast heart's delight,
I have sad heart's sorrow
For a false false maid
That will wed to-morrow.

'Tis all for a rose,
That I gave her not,
And I would that it grew
In the garden plot.

And I would the rose-tree
Were still to set,
That my love Marie
Might love me yet.

BALLADS OF MODERN GREECE

THE BRIGAND'S GRAVE

THE moon came up above the hill,
The sun went down the sea;
Go, maids, and fetch the well-water,
But, lad, come here to me.

Gird on my jack and my old sword,
For I have never a son;
And you must be the chief of all
When I am dead and gone.

But you must take my old broad sword,
And cut the green bough of the tree,
And strew the green boughs on the ground
To make a soft death bed for me,

And you must bring the holy priest
That I may sained be;
For I have lived a roving life
Fifty years under the greenwood tree.

And you shall make a grave for me,
And make it deep and wide;
That I may turn about and dream
With my old gun by my side.

And leave a window to the east,
And the swallows will bring the spring;

And all the merry month of May
The nightingales will sing.

THE SUDDEN BRIDAL

IT was a maid lay sick of love,
All for a leman fair;
And it was three of her bower-maidens
That came to comfort her.

The first she bore a blossomed branch,
The second an apple brown,
The third she had a silk kerchief,
And still her tears ran down.

The first she mocked, the second she laughed—
" We have loved lemans fair,
We made our hearts like the iron stone
Had little teen or care."

" If ye have loved 'twas a false false love,
And an ill leman was he;
But her true love had angel's eyes,
And as fair was his sweet body.

" And I will gird my green kirtle,
And braid my yellow hair,
And I will over the high hills
And bring her love to her."

" Nay, if you braid your yellow hair,
You'll twine my love from me."
" Now nay, now nay, my lady good,

That ever this should be !"

" When you have crossed the western hills
My true love you shall meet,
With a green flag blowing over him,
And green grass at his feet."

She has crossed over the high hills,
And the low hills between,
And she has found the may's leman
Beneath a flag of green.

'Twas four and twenty ladies fair
Were sitting on the grass;
But he has turned and looked on her,
And will not let her pass.

" You've maidens here, and maidens there,
And loves through all the land;
But what have you made of the lady fair
You gave the rose-garland ? "

" She was so harsh and cold of love,
To me gave little grace;
She wept if I but touched her hand,
Or kissed her bonny face.

" Yea, crows shall build in the eagle's nest,
The hawk the dove shall wed,
Before my old true love and I
Meet in one wedding bed."
When she had heard his bitter rede
That was his old true love,

She sat and wept within her bower,
And moaned even as a dove.

She rose up from her window seat,
And she looked out to see;
Her love came riding up the street
With a goodly company.

He was clad on with Venice gold,
Wrought upon cramoisie,
His yellow hair shone like the sun
About his fair body.

"Now shall I call him blossomed branch
That has ill knots therein ?
Or shall I call him basil plant,
That comes of an evil kin ?

" Oh, I shall give him goodly names,
My sword of damask fine;
My silver flower, my bright-winged bird,
Where go you, lover mine ? "

" I go to marry my new bride,
That I bring o'er the down;
And you shall be her bridal maid,
And hold her bridal crown."

" When you come to the bride chamber
Where your fair maiden is,
 You'll tell her I was fair of face,
But never tell her this,

" That still my lips were lips of love,
My kiss love's spring-water,
That my love was a running spring,
My breast a garden fair.

" And you have kissed the lips of love
And drained the well-water,
And you have spoiled the running spring,
And robbed the fruits so fair."

" Now he that will may scatter nuts,
And he may wed that will;
But she that was my old true love
Shall be my true love still."

GREEK FOLK SONGS

IANNOULA

ALL the maidens were merry and wed
All to lovers so fair to see;
The lover I took to my bridal bed
He is not long for love and me.
I spoke to him and he nothing said,
I gave him bread of the wheat so fine,
He did not eat of the bridal bread,
He did not drink of the bridal wine.
I made him a bed was soft and deep,
I made him a bed to sleep with me;
" Look on me once before you sleep,
And look on the flower of my fair body.

" Flowers of April, and fresh May-dew,
Dew of April and buds of May;
Two white blossoms that bud for you,
Buds that blossom before the day."

THE TELL-TALES

ALL in the mirk midnight when I was beside you,
Who has seen, who has heard, what was said, what was done ?
'Twas the night and the light of the stars that espied you,
The fall of the moon, and the dawning begun.
'Tis a swift star has fallen, a star that discovers
To the sea what the green sea has told to the oars,
And the oars to the sailors, and they of us lovers
Go singing this song at their mistress's doors.

TWILIGHT ON TWEED

THREE crests against the saffron sky,
Beyond the purple plain,
The dear remembered melody
Of Tweed once more again.

Wan water from the border hills,
Dear voice from the old years,
Thy distant music lulls and stills,
And moves to quiet tears.

Like a loved ghost thy fabled flood
Fleets through the dusky land;
Where Scott, come home to die, has stood,
 My feet returning stand.

A mist of memory broods and floats,
The border waters flow;
The air is full of ballad notes,
Borne out of long ago.

Old songs that sung themselves to me,
Sweet through a boy's day dream,
While trout below the blossom'd tree
Plashed in the golden stream.

Twilight, and Tweed, and Eildon Hill,
Fair and thrice fair you be;
You tell me that the voice is still
That should have welcomed me.

ONE FLOWER

" Up there shot a lily red,
With a patch of earth from the land of the dead,
For she was strong in the land of the dead"."
WHEN autumn suns are soft, and sea winds moan,
And golden fruits make sweet the golden air,
In gardens where the apple blossoms were,
In these old springs before I walked alone;
I pass among the pathways overgrown,
Of all the former flowers that kissed your feet
Remains a poppy, pallid from the heat,
A wild poppy that the wild winds have sown.
Alas ! the rose forgets your hands of rose;
The lilies slumber in the lily bed;
Tis only poppies in the dreamy close,
The changeless, windless garden of the dead,

You tend, with buds soft as your kiss that lies
In over happy dreams, upon mine eyes.

METEMPSYCHOSIS

I SHALL not see thee, nay, but I shall know
Perchance, thy grey eyes in another's eyes,
Shall guess thy curls in gracious locks that flow
On purest brows, yea, and the swift surmise
Shall follow, and track, and find thee in disguise
Of all sad things, and fair, where sunsets glow,
When through the scent of heather, faint and low,
The weak wind whispers to the day that dies.

From all sweet art, and out of all " old rhyme,"
Thine eyes and lips are light and song to me;
The shadows of the beauty of all time,
Carven and sung, are only shapes of thee;
Alas, the shadowy shapes ! ah, sweet my dear,
Shall life or death bring all thy being near ?

LOST IN HADES

I DREAMED that somewhere in the shadowy place,
Grief of farewell unspoken was forgot
In welcome, and regret remembered not;
And hopeless prayer accomplished turned to praise
On lips that had been songless many days;
Hope had no more to hope for, and desire
And dread were overpast, in white attire
New born we walked among the new world's ways.

Then from the press of shades a spirit threw
Towards me such apples as these gardens bear;
And turning, I was 'ware of her, and knew
And followed her fleet voice and flying hair,—
Followed, and found her not, and seeking you
I found you never, dearest, anywhere.

A STAR IN THE NIGHT

THE perfect piteous beauty of thy face,
Is like a star the dawning drives away;
Mine eyes may never see in the bright day
Thy pallid halo, thy supernal grace:
But in the night from forth the silent place
Thou comest, dim in dreams, as doth a stray
Star of the starry flock that in the grey
Is seen, and lost, and seen a moment's space.

And as the earth at night turns to a star,
Loved long ago, and dearer than the sun,
So in the spiritual place afar,
At night our souls are mingled and made one,
And wait till one night fall, and one dawn rise,
That brings no noon too splendid for your eyes.

A SUNSET ON YARROW

THE wind and the day had lived together,
They died together, and far away
Spoke farewell in the sultry weather,
Out of the sunset, over the heather,
The dying wind and the dying day.

Far in the south, the summer Levin
Flushed, a flame in the grey soft air:
We seemed to look on the hills of heaven;
You saw within, but to me 'twas given
To see your face, as an angel's, there.
Never again, ah surely never
Shall we wait and watch, where of old we stood,
The low good-night of the hill and the river,
The faint light fade, and the wan stars quiver,
Twain grown one in the solitude.

HESPEROTHEN

BY the example of certain Grecian mariners, who, being safely returned from
the war about Troy, leave yet again their own lands and gods, seeking they know
not what, and choosing neither to abide in the fair Phæacian island, nor to dwell
and die with the Sirens, at length end miserably in a desert country by the sea, is
set forth the Vanity of Melancholy. And by the land of Phæacia is to be understood
the place of Art and of fair Pleasures; and by Circe's Isle, the places of bodily de-
lights, whereof men, falling aweary, attain to Eld, and to the darkness of that age.
Which thing Master Françoys Rabelais feigned, under the similitude of the Isle of
the Macræones.

THE SEEKERS FOR PHÆACIA

THERE is a land in the remotest day,
Where the soft night is born, and sunset dies;
The eastern shores see faint tides fade away,
That wash the lands where laughter, tears, and sighs,
Make life,—the lands beneath the blue of common skies.

But in the west is a mysterious sea,
(What sails have seen it, or what shipmen known ?)
With coasts enchanted where the Sirens be,
With islands where a Goddess walks alone,
And in the cedar trees the magic winds make moan.

Eastward the human cares of house and home,
Cities, and ships, and unknown Gods, and loves;
Westward, strange maidens fairer than the foam,
And lawless lives of men, and haunted groves,
Wherein a God may dwell, and where the Dryad roves.

The Gods are careless of the days and death
Of toilsome men, beyond the western seas;
The Gods are heedless of their painful breath,
And love them not, for they are not as these;
But in the golden west they live and lie at ease.

Yet the Phæacians well they love, who live
At the light's limit, passing careless hours,
Most like the Gods; and they have gifts to give,
Even wine, and fountains musical, and flowers,
And song, and if they will, swift ships, and magic powers.

It is a quiet midland.; in the cool
Of twilight comes the God, though no man prayed,
To watch the maids and young men beautiful
Dance, and they see him, and are not afraid,
For they are near of kin to Gods, and un-dismayed.

Ah, would the bright red prows might bring us nigh
The dreamy isles that the Immortals keep!
But with a mist they hide them wondrously,

And far the path and dim to where they sleep,—
The loved, the shadowy lands along the shadowy deep.

A SONG OF PHJEACIA

THE languid sunset, mother of roses,
Lingers, a light on the magic seas,
The wide fire flames, as a flower uncloses,
Heavy with odour, and loose to the breeze.

The red rose clouds, without law or leader,
Gather and float in the airy plain;
The nightingale sings to the dewy cedar,
The cedar scatters his scent to the main.

The strange flowers' perfume turns to singing,
Heard afar over moonlit seas;
The Siren's song, grown faint in winging,
Falls in scent on the cedar trees.

As waifs blown out of the sunset, flying,
Purple, and rosy, and grey, the birds
Brighten the air with their wings; their
crying Wakens a moment the weary herds.

Butterflies flit from the fairy garden,
 Living blossoms of flying flowers;
Never the nights with winter harden,
Nor moons wax keen in this land of ours.

Great fruits, fragrant, green and golden,
Gleam in the green, and droop and fall;
Blossom, and bud, and flower unfolden,

Swing, and cling to the garden wall.

Deep in the woods as twilight darkens,
Glades are red with the scented fire;
Far in the dells the white maid hearkens,
Song and sigh of the heart's desire.

Ah, and as moonlight fades in morning,
Maiden's song in the matin grey,
Faints as the first bird's note, a warning,
Wakes and wails to the new-born day.
The waking song and the dying measure
Meet, and the waxing and waning light
Meet, and faint with the hours of pleasure,
The rose of the sea and the sky is white.

THE DEPARTURE FROM PHÆACIA

THE PHÆACIANS

WHY from the dreamy meadows,
More fair than any dream,
Why will you seek the shadows
Beyond the ocean stream ?

Through straits of storm and peril,
Through firths unsailed before,
Why make you for the sterile,
The dark Kimmerian shore ?

There no bright streams are flowing,
There day and night are one,

No harvest time, no sowing,
No sight of any sun;

No sound of song or tabor,
No dance shall greet you there;
No noise of mortal labour,
Breaks on the blind chill air.

Are ours not happy places,
Where Gods with mortals trod ?
Saw not our sires the faces
Of many a present God ?

THE SEEKERS

NAY, now no God comes hither,
In shape that men may see;
They fare we know not whither,
We know not what they be.

Yea, though the sunset lingers
Far in your fairy glades,
Though yours the sweetest singers,
Though yours the kindest maids,

Yet here be the true shadows,
Here in the doubtful light;
Amid the dreamy meadows
No shadow haunts the night.

We seek a city splendid,
With light beyond the sun;
Or lands where dreams are ended,

And works and days are done.

A BALLAD OF DEPARTURE [2]

FAIR white bird, what song art thou singing
In wintry weather of lands o'er sea ?
Dear white bird, what way art thou winging,
Where no grass grows, and no green tree ?

I looked at the far off fields and grey,
There grew no tree but the cypress tree,
That bears sad fruits with the flowers of May,
And whoso looks on it, woe is he.

And whoso eats of the fruit thereof
Has no more sorrow, and no more love;
And who sets the same in his garden stead,
In a little space he is waste and dead.

    [2] From the Romaic.

THEY HEAR THE SIRENS FOR THE SECOND TIME

THE weary sails a moment slept,
The oars were silent for a space,
As past Hesperian shores we swept,
That were as a remembered face
Seen after lapse of hopeless years,
In Hades, when the shadows meet,
Dim through the mist of many tears,
And strange, and though a shadow, sweet.

So seemed the half-remembered shore,

That slumbered, mirrored in the blue,
With havens where we touched of yore,
And ports that over well we knew.

Then broke the calm before a breeze
That sought the secret of the west;
And listless all we swept the seas
Towards the Islands of the Blest.

Beside a golden sanded bay
We saw the Sirens, very fair
The flowery hill whereon they lay,
The flowers set upon their hair.
Their old sweet song came down the wind,
Remembered music waxing strong,
Ah now no need of cords to bind,
No need had we of Orphic song.

It once had seemed a little thing,
To lay our lives down at their feet,
That dying we might hear them sing,
And dying see their faces sweet;

But now, we glanced, and passing by,
No care had we to tarry long;
Faint hope, and rest, and memory
Were more than any Siren's song.

CIRCE'S ISLE REVISITED

AH, Circe, Circe ! in the wood we cried;
Ah, Circe, Circe! but no voice replied ;
No voice from bowers o'ergrown and ruinous

As fallen rocks upon the mountain side.

There was no sound of singing in the air;
Faded or fled the maidens that were fair,
No more for sorrow or joy were seen of us,
No light of laughing eyes, or floating hair.

The perfume, and the music, and the flame
Had passed away ; the memory of shame
Alone abode, and stings of faint desire,
And pulses of vague quiet went and came.

Ah, Circe ! in thy sad changed fairy place,
Our dead Youth came and looked on us a space,
With drooping wings, and eyes of faded fire,
And wasted hair about a weary face.

Why had we ever sought the magic isle
That seemed so happy in the days erewhile ?
Why did we ever leave it, where we met
A world of happy wonders in one smile ?

Back to the westward and the waning light
We turned, we fled; the solitude of night
Was better than the infinite regret,
In fallen places of our dead delight.

THE LIMIT OF LANDS

BETWEEN the circling ocean sea
And the poplars of Persephone
There lies a strip of barren sand,
Flecked with the sea's last spray, and

strown
With waste leaves of the poplars, blown
From gardens of the shadow land.

With altars of old sacrifice
The shore is set, in mournful wise
The mists upon the ocean brood;
Between the water and the air
The clouds are born that float and fare
Between the water and the wood.

Upon the grey sea never sail
Of mortals passed within our hail,
Where the last weak waves faint and flow;
We heard within the poplar pale
The murmur of a doubtful wail
Of voices loved so long ago.

We scarce had care to die or live,
We had no honey cake to give,
No wine of sacrifice to shed;
There lies no new path over sea,
And now we know how faint they be,
The feasts and voices of the Dead.

Ah, flowers and dance ! ah, sun and snow!
Glad life, sad life we did forego
To dream of quietness and rest;
Ah, would the fleet sweet roses here
Poured light and perfume through the drear
Pale year, and wan land of the west.

Sad youth, that let the spring go by

Because the spring is swift to fly,
Sad youth, that feared to mourn or love,
Behold how sadder far is this,
To know that rest is nowise bliss,
And darkness is the end thereof.

COLINETTE

FOR A SKETCH BY MR. G. LESLIE, A.R.A.

FRANCE your country, as we know;
Room enough for guessing yet,
What lips now or long ago,
Kissed and named you—Colinette.
In what fields from sea to sea,
By what stream your home was set,
Loire or Seine was glad of thee,
Marne or Rhone, O Colinette ?

Did you stand with " maidens ten,
Fairer maids were never seen,"
When the young king and his men
Passed among the orchards green ?

Nay, old ballads have a note
Mournful, we would fain forget;
No such sad old air should float
Round your young brows, Colinette.

Say, did Ronsard sing to you,
Shepherdess, to lull his pain,
When the court went wandering through
Rose pleasances of Touraine ?

Ronsard and his famous Rose
Long are dust the breezes fret;
You, within the garden close,
You are blooming, Colinette.

Have I seen you proud and gay,
With a patched and perfumed beau,
Dancing through the summer day,
Misty summer of Watteau ?
Nay, so sweet a maid as you
Never walked a minuet
With the splendid courtly crew;
Nay, forgive me, Colinette.

Not from Greuze's canvasses
Did you cast a glance, a smile;
You are not as one of these,
Yours is beauty without guile.
Round your maiden brows and hair
Maidenhood and Childhood met
Crown and kiss you, sweet and fair,
New art's blossom, Colinette.

A SUNSET OF WATTEAU

LUI

THE silk sail fills, the soft winds wake,
Arise and tempt the seas;
Our ocean is the Palace lake,
Our waves the ripples that we make
Among the mirrored trees.

ELLE

Nay, sweet the shore, and sweet the song,
And dear the languid dream;
The music mingled all day long
With paces of the dancing throng,
And murmur of the stream.

An hour ago, an hour ago,
We rested in the shade;
And now, why should we seek to know
What way the wilful waters flow ?
There is no fairer glade.

LUI

Nay, pleasure flits, and we must sail,
And seek him everywhere;
Perchance in sunset's golden pale
He listens to the nightingale,
Amid the perfumed air.

Come, he has fled; you are not you,
And I no more am I;
Delight is changeful as the hue
Of heaven, that is no longer blue
In yonder sunset sky.

Nay, if we seek we shall not find,
If we knock none openeth;
Nay, see, the sunset fades behind
The mountains, and the cold night wind
Blows from the house of Death.

A NATIVITY OF SANDRO BOTTICELLI

" WROUGHT in the troublous times of Italy
By Sandro Botticelli," when for fear
Of that last judgment, and last day drawn near
To end all labour and all revelry,
He worked and prayed in silence; this is she
That by the holy cradle sees the bier,
And in spice gifts the hyssop on the spear,
And out of Bethlehem, Gethsemane.

Between the gold sky and the green o'er head,
The twelve great shining angels, garlanded,
Marvel upon this face, wherein combine
The mother's love that shone on all of us,
And maiden rapture that makes luminous
The brows of Margaret and Catherine.

TWO HOMES

To a young English lady in the Hospital of the Wounded at Carlsruhe, Sept.
1870

WHAT does the dim gaze of the dying find
To waken dream or memory, seeing you ?
In your sweet eyes what other eyes are blue,
And in your hair what gold hair on the wind
Floats of the days gone almost out of mind ?
In deep green valleys of the Fatherland
He may remember girls with locks like thine;
May dream how, where the waiting angels stand,

Some lost love's eyes are dim before they shine
With welcome :—so past homes, or homes to be,
He sees a moment, ere, a moment blind,
He crosses Death's inhospitable sea,
And with brief passage of those barren lands
Comes to the home that is not made with hands.

SUMMER'S ENDING

THE flags below the shadowy fern
Shine like spears between sun and sea,
The tide and the summer begin to turn,
And ah, for hearts, for hearts that yearn,
For fires of autumn that catch and burn,
For love gone out between thee and me.

The wind is up, and the weather broken,
Blue seas, blue eyes, are grieved and grey,
Listen, the word that the wind has spoken,
Listen, the sound of the sea,—a token
That summer's over, and troths are broken,—
That loves depart as the hours decay.

Λ love has passed to the loves passed over,
A month has fled to the months gone by;
And none may follow, and none recover
July and June, and never a lover
May stay the wings of the Loves that hover,
As fleet as the light in a sunset sky.

NIGHTINGALE WEATHER

" Serai-je nonnette, oui ou non ?
Serai-je nonnette ? je crois que non.
Derrière chez mon père
Il est un bois taillis,
Le rossignol y chante
Et le jour et le nuit.
Il chante pour les filles
Qui n'ont pas d'ami;
Il ne chante pas pour moi,
J'en ai un, Dieu merci."

OLD FRENCH.

I'LL never be a nun, I trow,
While apple bloom is white as snow,
But far more fair to see;
I'll never wear nun's black and white
While nightingales make sweet the night
Within the apple tree.

Ah, listen ! 'tis the nightingale,
And in the wood he makes his wail,
Within the apple tree;
He singeth of the sore distress
Of many ladies loverless;
Thank God, no song for me.

For when the broad May moon is low,
A gold fruit seen where blossoms blow
In the boughs of the apple tree,
A step I know is at the gate;

Ah love, but it is long to wait
Until night's noon bring thee!

Between lark's song and nightingale's
A silent space, while dawning pales,
The birds leave still and free
For words and kisses musical,
For silence and for sighs that fall
In the dawn, 'twixt him and me.

LOVE AND WISDOM

" When last we gathered roses in the garden I found my wits, but truly you lost yours."

THE BROKEN HEART.

JULY and June brought flowers and love
To you, but I would none thereof,
Whose heart kept all through summer time
A flower of frost and winter rime.
Yours was true wisdom—was it not ?—
Even love; but I had clean forgot,
Till seasons of the falling leaf,
All loves, but one that turned to grief.
At length at touch of autumn tide,
When roses fell, and summer died,
All in a dawning deep with dew,
Love flew to me, love fled from you.
The roses drooped their weary heads,
I spoke among the garden beds;

You would not hear, you could not know,

Summer and love seemed long ago,
As far, as faint, as dim a dream,
As to the dead this world may seem.
Ah sweet, in winter's miseries,
Perchance you may remember this,
How wisdom was not justified
In summer time or autumn-tide,
Though for this once below the sun,
Wisdom and love were made at one;
But love was bitter-bought enough,
And wisdom light of wing as love.

GOOD-BYE

Kiss me, and say good-bye;
Good-bye, there is no word to say but
this,
Nor any lips left for my lips to kiss,
Nor any tears to shed, when these tears
dry;
Kiss me, and say, good-bye.

Farewell, be glad, forget;
There is no need to say "forget," I
know,
For youth is youth, and time will have
it so,
And though your lips are pale, and your eyes
wet,
Farewell, you must forget.

You shall bring home your sheaves,
Many, and heavy, and with blossoms twined

Of memories that go not out of mind;
Let this one sheaf be twined with poppy leaves
When you bring home your sheaves.

In garnered loves of thine,
The ripe good fruit of many hearts and
years,
Somewhere let this lie, grey and salt with tears;
It grew too near the sea wind, and the brine
Of life, this love of mine.

This sheaf was spoiled in spring,
And over-long was green, and early sere,
And never gathered gold in the late year
From autumn suns, and moons of harvesting,
But failed in frosts of spring.

Yet was it thine, my sweet,
This love, though weak as young corn withered,
Whereof no man may gather and make bread;
Thine, though it never knew the summer heat;
Forget not quite, my sweet.

AN OLD PRAYER

ODYSSEY, xiii. 59
MY prayer an old prayer borroweth,
Of ancient love and memory—
" Do thou farewell, till Eld and Death,
That come to all men, come to thee."
Gently as winter's early breath,
Scarce felt, what time the swallows flee,
To lands whereof no man knoweth

Of summer, over land and sea;
So with thy soul may summer be,
Even as the ancient singer saith,
" Do thou farewell, till Eld and Death,
That come to all men, come to thee."

LOVE'S MIRACLE

WITH other helpless folk about the gate,
The gate called Beautiful, with weary eyes
That take no pleasure in the summer skies,
Nor all things that are fairest, does she wait;
So bleak a time, so sad a changeless fate
Makes her with dull experience early wise,
And in the dawning and the sunset, sighs
That all hath been, and shall be, desolate.

Ah, if Love come not soon, and bid her live,
And know herself the fairest of fair things,
Ah, if he have no healing gift to give,
Warm from his breast, and holy from his wings,
Or if at least Love's shadow in passing by
Touch not and heal her, surely she must die.

DREAMS

HE spake not truth, however wise, who said
That happy, and that hapless men in sleep
Have equal fortune, fallen from care as deep
As countless, careless, races of the dead.
Not so, for alien paths of dreams we tread,
And one beholds the faces that he sighs

In vain to bring before his daylit eyes,
And waking, he remembers on his bed;

And one with fainting heart and feeble hand
Fights a dim battle in a doubtful land,
Where strength and courage were of no avail;
And one is borne on fairy breezes far
To the bright harbours of a golden star
Down fragrant fleeting waters rosy pale.

FAIRY LAND

IN light of sunrise and sunsetting,
The long days lingered, in forgetting
That ever passion, keen to hold
What may not tarry, was of old,
In lands beyond the weary wold;
Beyond the bitter stream whose flood
Runs red waist-high with slain men's blood.
Was beauty once a thing that died ?
Was pleasure never satisfied ?
Was rest still broken by the vain
Desire of action, bringing pain,
To die in languid rest again ?
All this was quite forgotten there,
Where never winter chilled the year,
Nor spring brought promise unfulfilled,
Nor, with the eager summer killed,

The languid days drooped autumnwards.
So magical a season guards
The constant prime of a cool June;
So slumbrous is the river's tune,

That knows no thunder of heavy rains,
Nor ever in the summer wanes,
Like waters of the summer time
In lands far from the Fairy clime.

Yea, there the Fairy maids are kind,
With nothing of the changeful mind
Of maidens in the days that were;
And if no laughter fills the air With sound of silver murmurings,
And if no prayer of passion brings
A love nigh dead to life again,
Yet sighs more subtly sweet remain,
And smiles that never satiate,
And loves that fear scarce any fate.

Alas, no words can bring the bloom
Of Fairy Land; the faint perfume,
The sweet low light, the magic air,
To eyes of who has not been there :
Alas, no words, nor any spell
Can lull the eyes that know too well,
The lost fair world of Fairy Land.

Ah, would that I had never been
The lover of the Fairy Queen !
Or would that through the sleepy town,
The grey old place of Ercildoune,
And all along the little street,
The soft fall of the white deer's feet
Came, with the mystical command
That I must back to Fairy Land!

TWO SONNETS OF THE SIRENS

"Les Sirènes estoient tant intimes amies et fidelles com-pagnes de Proserpine, qu'elles estoient toujours ensemble. Esmues du juste deuil de la perte de leur chère com pagne, et enuyèes jusques au desespoir, elles s'arrestérent à la mer Sicilienne, où par leurs chants elles attiroient les navigans, mais l'unique fin de la volupté de leur musique est la Mort."—PONTUS DE TYARD, 1570.

TWO SONNETS OF THE SIRENS

I

THE Sirens once were maidens innocent
That through the water-meads with Proserpine
Plucked no fire-hearted flowers, but were content
Cool fritillaries and flag-flowers to twine,
With lilies woven and with wet woodbine;
Till once they sought the bright Ætnæan flowers,
And their bright mistress fled from summer hours
With Hades, down the irremeable decline.
And they have sought her all the wide world
Through
Till many years, and wisdom, and much wrong
Have filled and changed their song, and o'er the blue
Rings deadly sweet the magic of the song,
And whoso hears must listen till he die
Far on the flowery shores of Sicily.

II

So is it with this singing art of ours,

That once with maids went maidenlike, and played
With woven dances in the poplar-shade,
And all her song was but of lady's bowers
And the returning swallows, and spring-flowers,
Till forth to seek a shadow-queen she strayed,
A shadowy land ; and now hath overweighed
Her singing chaplet with the snow and showers.
Yea, fair well-water for the bitter brine
She left, and by the margin of life's sea
Sings, and her song is full of the sea's moan,
And wild with dread, and love of Proserpine;
And whoso once has listened to her, he
His whole life long is slave to her alone.

À LA BELLE HÉLÈNE

AFTER RONSARD

MORE closely than the clinging vine
About the wedded tree,
Clasp thou thine arms, ah, mistress mine!
About the heart of me.
Or seem to sleep, and stoop your face
Soft on my sleeping eyes,
Breathe in your life, your heart, your grace,
Through me, in kissing wise.
Bow down, bow down your face, I pray,
To me, that swoon to death,
Breathe back the life you kissed away,
Breathe back your kissing breath.
So by your eyes I swear and say,
My mighty oath and sure,

From your kind arms no maiden may
My loving heart allure.

I'll bear your yoke, that's light enough,
And to the Elysian plain,
When we are dead of love, my love,
One boat shall bear us twain.
They'll flock around you, fleet and fair,
All true loves that have been,
And you of all the shadows there,
Shall be the shadow queen.
Ah, shadow-loves, and shadow-lips !
Ah, while 'tis called to-day,
Love me, my love, for summer slips,
And August ebbs away.

SYLVIE ET AURÈLIE

IN MEMORY OF GÉRARD DE NERVAL

Two loves there were, and one was born
Between the sunset and the rain;
Her singing voice went through the corn,
Her dance was woven 'neath the thorn,
On grass the fallen blossoms stain ;
And suns may set, and moons may wane,
But this love comes no more again.

There were two loves and one made white
Thy singing lips, and golden hair;
Born of the city's mire and light,

The shame and splendour of the night,
She trapped and fled thee unaware;
Not through the lamplight and the rain
Shalt thou behold this love again.

Go forth and seek, by wood and hill,
Thine ancient love of dawn and dew;
There comes no voice from mere or rill,
Her dance is over, fallen still
The ballad burdens that she knew;
And thou must wait for her in vain,
Till years bring back thy youth again.

That other love, afield, afar
Fled the light love, with lighter feet.
Nay, though thou seek where gravesteads are
And flit in dreams from star to star,
That dead love shalt thou never meet,
Till through bleak dawn and blowing rain
Thy fled soul find her soul again.

A LOST PATH

Plotinus, the Greek philosopher, had a certain proper mode of ecstasy, where-
by, as Porphyry saith, his soul, becoming free from his deathly flesh, was made one
with the Spirit that is in the World.

ALAS, the path is lost, we cannot leave
Our bright, our clouded life, and pass away
As through strewn clouds, that stain the quiet eve,
To heights remoter of the purer day.
The soul may not, returning whence she came,
Bathe herself deep in Being, and forget

The joys that fever, and the cares that fret,
Made once more one with the eternal flame
That breathes in all things ever more the same.
She would be young again, thus drinking deep
Of her old life; and this has been, men say,
But this we know not, who have only sleep
To soothe us, sleep more terrible than day,
Where dead delights, and fair lost faces stray,

To make us weary at our wakening;
And of that long-lost path to the Divine
We dream, as some Greek shepherd erst might sing,
Half credulous, of easy Proserpine,
And of the lands that lie " beneath the day's decline."

THE SHADE OF HELEN

Some say that Helen went never to Troy, but abode in Egypt; for the Gods, having made in her semblance a woman out of clouds and shadows, sent the same to be wife to Paris. For this shadow then the Greeks and Trojans slew each other.

WHY from the quiet hollows of the hills,
And extreme meeting place of light and shade,
Wherein soft rains fell slowly, and became
Clouds among sister clouds, where fair spent
Beams
And dying glories of the sun would dwell,
Why have they whom I know not, nor may know,
Strange hands, unseen and ruthless, fashioned me,
And borne me from the silent shadowy hills,
Hither, to noise and glow of alien life,
To harsh and clamorous swords, and sound of
war?

One speaks unto me words that would be sweet,
Made harsh, made keen with love that knows
me not,
And some strange force, within me or around,
Makes answer, kiss for kiss, and sigh for sigh,
And somewhere there is fever in the halls,
That troubles me, for no such trouble came
To vex the cool far hollows of the hills.

The foolish folk crowd round me, and they
cry, That house, and wife, and lands, and all Troy
town, Are little to lose, if they may keep me here,
And see me flit, a pale and silent shade,
Among the streets bereft, and helpless shrines.

At other hours another life seems mine,
Where one great river runs unswollen of rain,

By pyramids of unremembered kings,
And homes of men obedient to the Dead
There dark and quiet faces come and go
Around me, then again the shriek of arms,
And all the turmoil of the Ilian men.
What are they ? even shadows such as I.
What make they? Even this—the sport of
Gods—
The sport of Gods, however free they seem.
Ah would the game were ended, and the light,
The blinding light, and all too mighty suns, Withdrawn, and I once more with
sister shades,
Unloved, forgotten, mingled with the mist,
Dwelt in the hollows of the shadowy hills.

Ah, would 'twere the cloud's playtime, when the
Sun
Clothes us in raiment of a rosy flame,
And through the sky we flit, and gather grey,
Like men that leave their golden youth behind,

And through their wind-driven ways they gather
grey,
And we like them grow wan, and the chill East
Receives us, as the Earth accepts all men,—
But we await the dawn of a new day.

JACQUES TAHUREAU

I

JACQUES TAHUREAU, 1530

AH thou ! that, undeceived and unregretting,
Saw'st Death so near thee on the flowery way,
And with no sigh that life was near the
setting, Took'st the delight and dalliance of the day,
Happy thou wert, to live and pass away
Ere life or love had done thee any wrong;
Ere thy wreath faded, or thy locks grew grey,
Or summer came to lull thine April song,

Sweet as all shapes of sweet things unfulfilled,
Buds bloomless, and the broken violet,
The first spring days, the sounds and scents thereof;
So clear thy fire of song, so early chilled,
So brief, so bright thy life that gaily met

Death, for thy Death came hand in hand with Love.

FRANÇOIS VILLON

II

FRANÇOIS VILLON, 1450

. LIST, all that love light mirth, light tears, and all
That know the heart of shameful loves, or pure;
That know delights depart, desires endure,
A fevered tribe of ghosts funereal,
Widowed of dead delights gone out of call;
List, all that deem the glory of the rose
Is brief as last year's suns, or last year's snows
The new suns melt from off the sundial.

All this your master Villon knew and sung;
Despised delights, and faint foredone desire;
And shame, a deathless worm, a quenchless fire;
And laughter from the heart's last sorrow wrung,
When half-repentance but makes evil whole,
And prayer that cannot help wears out the soul.

III

PIERRE RONSARD, 1560

MASTER, I see thee with the locks of grey,
Crowned by the Muses with the laurel-wreath ;
I see the roses hiding underneath,
Cassandra's gift; she was less dear than they.
Thou, Master, first hast roused the lyric lay,
The sleeping song that the dead years
bequeath,
Hast sung sweet answer to the songs that breathe
Through ages, and through ages far away.

Yea, and in thee the pulse of ancient passion
Leaped, and the nymphs amid the spring-water

Made bare their lovely limbs in the old fashion,
And birds' song in the branches was astir.
Ah, but thy songs are sad, thy roses wan,
Thy bees have fed on yews Sardinian.

IV

GÉRARD DE NERVAL

OF all that were thy prisons—ah, untamed,
Ah, light and sacred soul!—none holds thee
now;
No wall, no bar, no body of flesh, but thou
Art free and happy in the lands unnamed,
About whose gates, with weary wings and maimed,
Thou most wert wont to linger, entering there
A moment, and returning rapt, with fair
Tidings that men or heeded not or blamed;
And they would smile and wonder, seeing where
Thou stood'st, to watch light leaves, or clouds? Or
wind, Dreamily murmuring a ballad air,
Caught from the Valois peasants; dost thou find
Old prophecies fulfilled now, old tales true
In the new world, where all things are made new ?

V

THE DEATH OF MIRANDOLA, 1494

"The Queen of Heaven appeared, comforting him and promising that he should not utterly die."—THOMAS MORE, *Life of Piens, Earl of Mirandola.*

STRANGE lilies came with autumn; new and old
Were mingling, and the old world passed
away,
And the night gathered, and the shadows grey
Dimmed the kind eyes and dimmed the locks of gold,
And face beloved of Mirandola.
The Virgin then, to comfort him and stay,
Kissed the thin cheek, and kissed the lips acold,
The lips unkissed of women many a day.

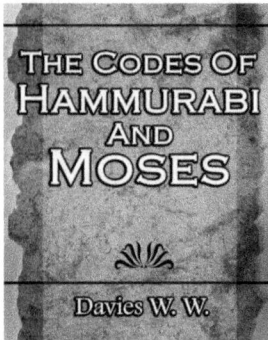

The Codes Of Hammurabi And Moses
W. W. Davies

QTY

The discovery of the Hammurabi Code is one of the greatest achievements of archaeology, and is of paramount interest, not only to the student of the Bible, but also to all those interested in ancient history...

Religion   **ISBN:** *1-59462-338-4*   **Pages:132**
MSRP $12.95

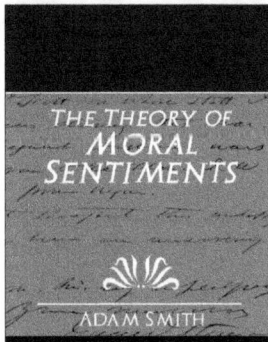

The Theory of Moral Sentiments
Adam Smith

QTY

This work from 1749. contains original theories of conscience amd moral judgment and it is the foundation for systemof morals.

Philosophy   **ISBN:** *1-59462-777-0*   **Pages:536**
MSRP $19.95

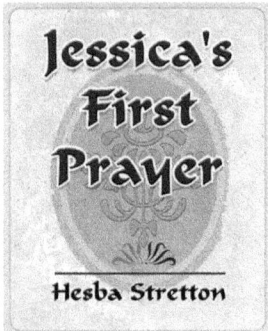

Jessica's First Prayer
Hesba Stretton

QTY

In a screened and secluded corner of one of the many railway-bridges which span the streets of London there could be seen a few years ago, from five o'clock every morning until half past eight, a tidily set-out coffee-stall, consisting of a trestle and board, upon which stood two large tin cans, with a small fire of charcoal burning under each so as to keep the coffee boiling during the early hours of the morning when the work-people were thronging into the city on their way to their daily toil...

Pages:84

Childrens   **ISBN:** *1-59462-373-2*   *MSRP $9.95*

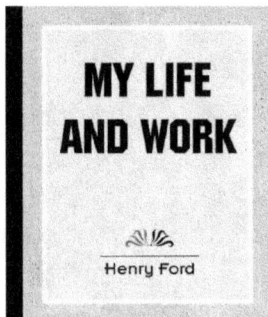

My Life and Work
Henry Ford

QTY

Henry Ford revolutionized the world with his implementation of mass production for the Model T automobile. Gain valuable business insight into his life and work with his own auto-biography... "We have only started on our development of our country we have not as yet, with all our talk of wonderful progress, done more than scratch the surface. The progress has been wonderful enough but..."

Pages:300

Biographies/   **ISBN:** *1-59462-198-5*   *MSRP $21.95*

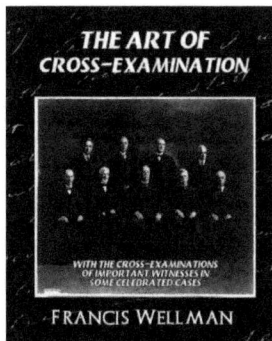

The Art of Cross-Examination
Francis Wellman

QTY

I presume it is the experience of every author, after his first book is published upon an important subject, to be almost overwhelmed with a wealth of ideas and illustrations which could readily have been included in his book, and which to his own mind, at least, seem to make a second edition inevitable. Such certainly was the case with me; and when the first edition had reached its sixth impression in five months, I rejoiced to learn that it seemed to my publishers that the book had met with a sufficiently favorable reception to justify a second and considerably enlarged edition. ..

Pages:412

Reference   ISBN: *1-59462-647-2*   *MSRP $19.95*

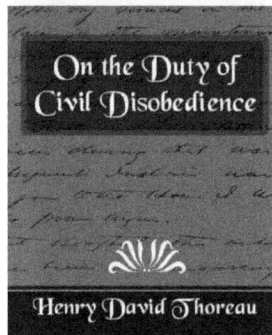

On the Duty of Civil Disobedience
Henry David Thoreau

QTY

Thoreau wrote his famous essay, On the Duty of Civil Disobedience, as a protest against an unjust but popular war and the immoral but popular institution of slave-owning. He did more than write—he declined to pay his taxes, and was hauled off to gaol in consequence. Who can say how much this refusal of his hastened the end of the war and of slavery ?

Law   ISBN: *1-59462-747-9*   **Pages:48**

MSRP $7.45

Dream Psychology Psychoanalysis for Beginners
Sigmund Freud

QTY

Sigmund Freud, born Sigismund Schlomo Freud (May 6, 1856 - September 23, 1939), was a Jewish-Austrian neurologist and psychiatrist who co-founded the psychoanalytic school of psychology. Freud is best known for his theories of the unconscious mind, especially involving the mechanism of repression; his redefinition of sexual desire as mobile and directed towards a wide variety of objects; and his therapeutic techniques, especially his understanding of transference in the therapeutic relationship and the presumed value of dreams as sources of insight into unconscious desires.

Pages:196

Psychology   ISBN: *1-59462-905-6*   *MSRP $15.45*

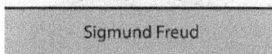

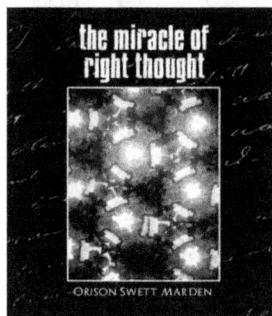

The Miracle of Right Thought
Orison Swett Marden

QTY

Believe with all of your heart that you will do what you were made to do. When the mind has once formed the habit of holding cheerful, happy, prosperous pictures, it will not be easy to form the opposite habit. It does not matter how improbable or how far away this realization may see, or how dark the prospects may be, if we visualize them as best we can, as vividly as possible, hold tenaciously to them and vigorously struggle to attain them, they will gradually become actualized, realized in the life. But a desire, a longing without endeavor, a yearning abandoned or held indifferently will vanish without realization.

Pages:360

Self Help   ISBN: *1-59462-644-8*   *MSRP $25.45*

The Rosicrucian Cosmo-Conception Mystic Christianity by *Max Heindel*   ISBN: *1-59462-188-8* **$38.95**
The Rosicrucian Cosmo-conception is not dogmatic, neither does it appeal to any other authority than the reason of the student. It is: not controversial, but is: sent forth in the, hope that it may help to clear...   New Age/Religion Pages 646

Abandonment To Divine Providence by *Jean-Pierre de Caussade*   ISBN: *1-59462-228-0* **$25.95**
"The Rev. Jean Pierre de Caussade was one of the most remarkable spiritual writers of the Society of Jesus in France in the 18th Century. His death took place at Toulouse in 1751. His works have gone through many editions and have been republished...   Inspirational/Religion Pages 400

Mental Chemistry by *Charles Haanel*   ISBN: *1-59462-192-6* **$23.95**
Mental Chemistry allows the change of material conditions by combining and appropriately utilizing the power of the mind. Much like applied chemistry creates something new and unique out of careful combinations of chemicals the mastery of mental chemistry...   New Age Pages 354

The Letters of Robert Browning and Elizabeth Barret Barrett 1845-1846 vol II   ISBN: *1-59462-193-4* **$35.95**
by *Robert Browning* and *Elizabeth Barrett*   Biographies Pages 596

Gleanings In Genesis (volume I) by *Arthur W. Pink*   ISBN: *1-59462-130-6* **$27.45**
Appropriately has Genesis been termed "the seed plot of the Bible" for in it we have, in germ form, almost all of the great doctrines which are afterwards fully developed in the books of Scripture which follow...   Religion/Inspirational Pages 420

The Master Key by *L. W. de Laurence*   ISBN: *1-59462-001-6* **$30.95**
In no branch of human knowledge has there been a more lively increase of the spirit of research during the past few years than in the study of Psychology, Concentration and Mental Discipline. The requests for authentic lessons in Thought Control, Mental Discipline and...   New Age/Business Pages 422

The Lesser Key Of Solomon Goetia by *L. W. de Laurence*   ISBN: *1-59462-092-X* **$9.95**
This translation of the first book of the "Lernegton" which is now for the first time made accessible to students of Talismanic Magic was done, after careful collation and edition, from numerous Ancient Manuscripts in Hebrew, Latin, and French...   New Age/Occult Pages 92

Rubaiyat Of Omar Khayyam by *Edward Fitzgerald*   ISBN:*1-59462-332-5* **$13.95**
Edward Fitzgerald, whom the world has already learned, in spite of his own efforts to remain within the shadow of anonymity, to look upon as one of the rarest poets of the century, was born at Bredfield, in Suffolk, on the 31st of March, 1809. He was the third son of John Purcell...   Music Pages 172

Ancient Law by *Henry Maine*   ISBN: *1-59462-128-4* **$29.95**
The chief object of the following pages is to indicate some of the earliest ideas of mankind, as they are reflected in Ancient Law, and to point out the relation of those ideas to modern thought.   Religion/History Pages 452

Far-Away Stories by *William J. Locke*   ISBN: *1-59462-129-2* **$19.45**
"Good wine needs no bush, but a collection of mixed vintages does. And this book is just such a collection. Some of the stories I do not want to remain buried for ever in the museum files of dead magazine-numbers an author's not unpardonable vanity..."   Fiction Pages 272

Life of David Crockett by *David Crockett*   ISBN: *1-59462-250-7* **$27.45**
"Colonel David Crockett was one of the most remarkable men of the times in which he lived. Born in humble life, but gifted with a strong will, an indomitable courage, and unremitting perseverance...   Biographies/New Age Pages 424

Lip-Reading by *Edward Nitchie*   ISBN: *1-59462-206-X* **$25.95**
Edward B. Nitchie, founder of the New York School for the Hard of Hearing, now the Nitchie School of Lip-Reading, Inc, wrote "LIP-READING Principles and Practice". The development and perfecting of this meritorious work on lip-reading was an undertaking...   How-to Pages 400

A Handbook of Suggestive Therapeutics, Applied Hypnotism, Psychic Science   ISBN: *1-59462-214-0* **$24.95**
by *Henry Munro*   Health/New Age/Health/Self-help Pages 376

A Doll's House: and Two Other Plays by *Henrik Ibsen*   ISBN: *1-59462-112-8* **$19.95**
Henrik Ibsen created this classic when in revolutionary 1848 Rome. Introducing some striking concepts in playwriting for the realist genre, this play has been studied the world over.   Fiction/Classics/Plays 308

The Light of Asia by *sir Edwin Arnold*   ISBN: *1-59462-204-3* **$13.95**
In this poetic masterpiece, Edwin Arnold describes the life and teachings of Buddha. The man who was to become known as Buddha to the world was born as Prince Gautama of India but he rejected the worldly riches and abandoned the reigns of power when...   Religion/History/Biographies Pages 170

The Complete Works of Guy de Maupassant by *Guy de Maupassant*   ISBN: *1-59462-157-8* **$16.95**
"For days and days, nights and nights, I had dreamed of that first kiss which was to consecrate our engagement, and I knew not on what spot I should put my lips..."   Fiction/Classics Pages 240

The Art of Cross-Examination by *Francis L. Wellman*   ISBN: *1-59462-309-0* **$26.95**
Written by a renowned trial lawyer, Wellman imparts his experience and uses case studies to explain how to use psychology to extract desired information through questioning.   How-to/Science/Reference Pages 408

Answered or Unanswered? by *Louisa Vaughan*   ISBN: *1-59462-248-5* **$10.95**
Miracles of Faith in China   Religion Pages 112

The Edinburgh Lectures on Mental Science (1909) by *Thomas*   ISBN: *1-59462-008-3* **$11.95**
This book contains the substance of a course of lectures recently given by the writer in the Queen Street Hall, Edinburgh. Its purpose is to indicate the Natural Principles governing the relation between Mental Action and Material Conditions...   New Age/Psychology Pages 148

Ayesha by *H. Rider Haggard*   ISBN: *1-59462-301-5* **$24.95**
Verily and indeed it is the unexpected that happens! Probably if there was one person upon the earth from whom the Editor of this, and of a certain previous history, did not expect to hear again...   Classics Pages 380

Ayala's Angel by *Anthony Trollope*   ISBN: *1-59462-352-X* **$29.95**
The two girls were both pretty, but Lucy who was twenty-one who supposed to be simple and comparatively unattractive, whereas Ayala was credited, as her Bombwhat romantic name might show, with poetic charm and a taste for romance, Ayala when her father died was nineteen...   Fiction Pages 484

The American Commonwealth by *James Bryce*   ISBN: *1-59462-286-8* **$34.45**
An interpretation of American democratic political theory. It examines political mechanics and society from the perspective of Scotsman James Bryce   Politics Pages 572

Stories of the Pilgrims by *Margaret P. Pumphrey*   ISBN: *1-59462-116-0* **$17.95**
This book explores pilgrims religious oppression in England as well as their escape to Holland and eventual crossing to America on the Mayflower, and their early days in New England...   History Pages 268

www.bookjungle.com *email: sales@bookjungle.com fax: 630-214-0564 mail: Book Jungle PO Box 2226 Champaign, IL 61825*

QTY

The Fasting Cure *by Sinclair Upton*   ISBN: *1-59462-222-1* **$13.95**
In the Cosmopolitan Magazine for May, 1910, and in the Contemporary Review (London) for April, 1910, I published an article dealing with my experiences in fasting. I have written a great many magazine articles, but never one which attracted so much attention... New Age/Self Help/Health Pages 164

Hebrew Astrology *by Sepharial*   ISBN: *1-59462-308-2* **$13.45**
In these days of advanced thinking it is a matter of common observation that we have left many of the old landmarks behind and that we are now pressing forward to greater heights and to a wider horizon than that which represented the mind-content of our progenitors... Astrology Pages 144

Thought Vibration or The Law of Attraction in the Thought World   ISBN: *1-59462-127-6* **$12.95**

by William Walker Atkinson   *Psychology/Religion Pages 144*

Optimism *by Helen Keller*   ISBN: *1-59462-108-X* **$15.95**
Helen Keller was blind, deaf, and mute since 19 months old, yet famously learned how to overcome these handicaps, communicate with the world, and spread her lectures promoting optimism. An inspiring read for everyone... Biographies/Inspirational Pages 84

Sara Crewe *by Frances Burnett*   ISBN: *1-59462-360-0* **$9.45**
In the first place, Miss Minchin lived in London. Her home was a large, dull, tall one, in a large, dull square, where all the houses were alike, and all the sparrows were alike, and where all the door-knockers made the same heavy sound... Childrens/Classic Pages 88

The Autobiography of Benjamin Franklin *by Benjamin Franklin*   ISBN: *1-59462-135-7* **$24.95**
The Autobiography of Benjamin Franklin has probably been more extensively read than any other American historical work, and no other book of its kind has had such ups and downs of fortune. Franklin lived for many years in England, where he was agent... Biographies/History Pages 332

Name	
Email	
Telephone	
Address	
City, State ZIP	

☐ **Credit Card**   ☐ **Check / Money Order**

Credit Card Number	
Expiration Date	
Signature	

Please Mail to: Book Jungle
PO Box 2226
Champaign, IL 61825
or Fax to: 630-214-0564

ORDERING INFORMATION
web: *www.bookjungle.com*
email: *sales@bookjungle.com*
fax: *630-214-0564*
mail: *Book Jungle PO Box 2226 Champaign, IL 61825*
or PayPal *to sales@bookjungle.com*

Please contact us for bulk discounts

DIRECT-ORDER TERMS

20% Discount if You Order
Two or More Books
Free Domestic Shipping!
Accepted: Master Card, Visa,
Discover, American Express